Joyful Mystery
…our story…

SYLVIA DAINS

Joyful Mystery
ISBN: Softcover 978-1-955581-30-1
Copyright © 2021 by Sylvia Dains

All rights reserved. No part of this book may be reproduced or transmitted in any form or by any means, electronic or mechanical, including photocopying, recording, or by any information storage and retrieval system, without permission in writing from the publisher.

Cover Art: *The Annunciation*, 1560s, Nosadella (Giovanni Francesco Bezzi), Italian, active ca.1549–1571. Oil on wood panel.

Parson's Porch Books is an imprint of Parson's Porch *&* Company (PP*&*C) in Cleveland, Tennessee. PP*&*C is an innovative organization which raises money by publishing books of noted authors, representing all genres. Its face and voice is **David Russell Tullock**

Parson's Porch *&* Company *turns books into bread & milk* by sharing its profits with the poor.

www.PARSONSPORCH.com

Joyful Mystery

…our story…

FOREWORD

How do you bring an age-old story to life in a modern moment? Only through investing much time, love, reflection, and prayer; because, as stated in the beginning, *everyone* knows the story. What more could there be to say about an event that has been re-told, re-studied, and re-sung over countless generations? So I looked for a way to express the familiar in fresh language, giving voice to the principal players; because who could be better at telling the story than the people who actually lived it?

This is not a story to be simply *read;* it's an invitation to ponder, to explore, to *inhale* the message it presents—until the message becomes such a part of us that we *breathe* it.

There are pauses in the story, places of sabbath, where the narrative is broken by poetic reflections to allow us to consider the journey and what it has to teach us: to simply *be present* to the journey as it unfolds and leads us from one step to the next. May the journey lead you gently…

PROLOGUE

This is a story we all know, one that could never have been envisioned by any one of *us* —a story we celebrate every year.

It's the saga of Light defeating darkness; of the divine Plan realized through the improbability of God's trusting and choosing *humans* to cooperate in bringing about events that could only be set in motion by the hand of God, who invariably chooses the unlikely to achieve the seemingly impossible.

We're *all* invited into the story, to find our place along the journey and discover where it leads. Not sure where to stand? Let me introduce you to our fellow travelers and their assigned roles:

Gabriel, who delivered the message
Zechariah, who learned the value of silence
Elizabeth, who never gave up
Mary, who pondered silently
Joseph, who dreamed and obeyed
The Innkeeper, who opened the door
The Star, lighting the way
The angel choir, leading the praise
Shepherds, who followed the Light
Herod, who schemed and murdered
The Magi, drawn *by* the light *to* the Light

Simeon, who waited…and waited…

Anna, who knew it all along…

and Jesus!—our Hope Incarnate!!

…and while Simeon waits and Mary ponders…while Joseph dreams and the world wonders…

God's hand is quietly, secretly at work: slowly and patiently drawing together the people and circumstances that will become the enfleshment of God's Word, spoken and realized:

> God from God, Light from Light, true God from true God… one in being with the Father, born of the Light to be Light for us:
>
> a Baby whose name is **"I AM!"**
>   Let us be on the way…

IN THE BEGINNING ...

World pregnant:
waiting for the Word,
hungering for the Word ...
stirring ...
deep in God's imagination.

Word
waiting to be spoken,
eager to be heard
waiting for Spirit's breath
to deliver souls from bondage;
to proclaim the saving Word...
growing...deep in God's imagination.

World
weary with its fighting
broken in spirit, heavy of heart—
one dark and dismal night
laid down its weapons
opened its arms to the
heavens, cried out its anguish:

"HOW LONG?"

God heard earth's cries,
knew the time was right to send
the long-awaited message:

"GABRIEL!"

"I have a task for you!"

GABRIEL

…waiting to be sent, eager to get to work…

…chosen to announce God's intention to a people yearning to hear God's voice; called to *be* that voice in their silence, declaring that *they* are the chosen instruments through which God will carry out the divine Promise made so long ago, the ancient covenant awaiting fulfillment:

> The Word of God: spoken,
> enfleshed—lived!!

Gabriel contemplates the implications of the trust placed in him by the Master. It's an awesome responsibility, one that offers endless, life-changing potential to those selected to share in the realization of the Promise as they live out their roles in bringing God's Word to fruition.

"I am entrusted to declare to these chosen ones words that will change their lives and order their actions for all of history.

How will they respond?
Will they even believe me?
What will be the immediate and long-term consequences of a 'Yes'??'

With this in mind, Gabriel sets out to help launch a story that will live throughout the ages; a story that will remind future generations of a time in history when God the Almighty chose limited humans to collaborate in the living and the telling of God's infinite, unlimited love for, and trust in, humankind.

ZECHARIAH SPEECHLESS!!

I was performing my duties in the temple, tending to the tasks entrusted to my care, when I was surprised to see that someone — a stranger — had slipped in without my notice. I greeted him, and we exchanged pleasantries; and as I moved to return to my duties, he announced to me that Elizabeth, my wife of many years, was with child!

Of course I was shocked, and explained to him that Elizabeth is well past child-bearing age. So many years we hoped and prayed for the blessing of a child, to no avail. Now we are old, and all hope is behind us; there's simply *no* chance that anything so farfetched could possibly be true.

As I argue with the visitor, trying to make him understand that his errand is hopeless, he assures me that it is *God* who sends the message: the announcement that Elizabeth will indeed give birth to a child — a son!— who will become a lone voice crying out into the wilderness:

"Prepare! the reign of God is near!"

...and that voice? It will be the voice of one named John...

—my son!—

whose mission will be to *announce* the Light, though not himself the Light. But because I have argued, because I have not believed, *my* voice will be silenced until the day of his birth.

Though I am bursting to shout from the housetops the wonder of this gift, my doubts have stilled my voice. I am sentenced to be mute — to tell *no one* of this wonder— to simply wait and listen for God's voice in the silence.

My tongue may be silent, but my spirit soars!!

ELIZABETH

All my life I've been faithful to my heritage as a daughter of Israel, following God's commands and recognizing the importance of living within them.

Of all that I've experienced in life, the most painful has been the fact of my barrenness. For as long as I can remember, my arms have ached to offer refuge and comfort to a baby, one in whom Zechariah could take pride —a *son* to carry on the name and heritage of his father. In this respect I feel a sense of failure:

> *Why* have I not been found worthy to be a mother?

Sadly, it's too late now: I am beyond the age of child-bearing. The women think I don't hear them mocking and laughing at me; but I hear it all, feel it deeply, and bear it quietly.

> Still, I can't help wondering….

I've had a visitor! — a stranger, who has announced to me that there *will* be a son, one destined to be the messenger — in the spirit and power of Elijah! — to prepare a people and clear the way for the coming of the promised One.

Elizabeth celebrates the removal of her curse as she anticipates the wonder to come: *"So has the Lord… taken away my disgrace…"*

*Listen to the angel speaking
to a virgin humbly kneeling
"Will you mother earth's redemption,
birth the Savior of the nations?"
Mary ponders, full of wonder:
softly whispers
"Let it be."*

MARY

"So much to do today! It will probably take me most of the day to get everything done— I'd better start right now!"

Mary is busy about many things today; and as she moves from one task to the next, she becomes aware that she is not alone; a presence has joined her, a stranger, who greets her:

"Good day, Mary, woman of grace! The Lord is with you! Among all women you are most blessed; and blessed too is the child you will bear."

Mary is stunned: *a child?*

Who is this visitor? Where does he come from? Who is this child he speaks of—and how should I respond to this strange greeting? I'm still inexperienced in certain worldly matters; and though I'm pledged to Joseph, I don't yet completely understand the fullness of what a marriage covenant requires or demands.

To the stranger she says: "I have no experience with a man; how is this possible?"

The visitor explains that I will conceive through the power of the Holy Spirit, and the child will be called the Son of God. He also *gives me the wonderful news that* *my cousin Elizabeth is six months pregnant!— adding that "**Nothing** is impossible for God."*

> *This is a lot to absorb:*
> *the "Son of God?"*

Elizabeth pregnant long after her allotted time for birthing has passed?

Can I believe this? What does it all mean?
Who is this child the presence speaks of?
*Why would God choose **me** for such a task?*

> ***A BABY!!***
> *Could **I** be a mother?*

> *What if I say "Yes"?*
> *What is the cost of "Yes"?*
> *What would Joseph think of me?*
> *We are betrothed, bound under the law to*
> *one another, and this would be considered*
> *adultery and reason for public censure.*

*What about Joseph's reputation, his standing among the other men?—among his friends? How could he be expected to understand this, when I don't understand it myself? What could this do to **his** life; and how would it affect our life together?*

*And what about **my** family, especially my father? — the scandal — the shame? After this, how will he be able to hold his head up among his friends? How many will look at him the same way, think of him the same way, after this?*

This is a difficult decision as I consider all of these matters, knowing that there must be others that I haven't yet thought of.

> *What if I say **"NO"**?*
> *Surely God could choose another:*
> *—but—*
> *if this is **really** God,*
> *how **can** I say "no?"*

*Even as I struggle with the message, I wonder how much strength my hesitation has if it's really GOD doing the asking…but then the visitor tells me that GOD is with me; that **nothing** is impossible!*

*Somehow, I am reassured: if this is **God's** plan and **God's** will, then it will be **God** who blesses it and brings it to fulfillment in ways I can't imagine.*

Having listened…having considered…I decide to trust the visitor's message and place myself before God's mercy:

> "I am the servant of the Lord; let it be as you say."

Joseph, of the House of David, whose lineage traces back to Abraham through forty- two generations....

JOSEPH

Joseph: silent….thoughtful…

Wherever he is mentioned in the story, we do not hear him speak. He is known to be a skilled artisan whose medium is wood: whose craft — the work of his hands — is his only statement.

Joseph: wordless….strong…faithful…

This has been a long day, and now in the silence of the evening, Joseph is tired and settles quickly into a deep sleep.

And then—a voice is saying, "Don't be afraid; this is of God."
—a dream?
—or did a stranger come to me, announce that I'm the one to parent the Almighty's son?

Could it be so? Mary—with child? People will talk; what will they say? What can I say to her father? How can I live with the disgrace?

I could expose her to the law; and she could be stoned and die a harlot's death; and I would be within my rights.

But—I could never let that happen to her; I love her. And think of it: a child entrusted to my care:
—A SON!!
*—someone to love, to teach; someone
to carry on the family business.*

*But **this** child —**this** son— is not my flesh, but born of the Almighty.
No matter how much I love him, how much I wish he were really my own—he is not — and never can be — **MY** son.*

How am I to feel about that?

How can I live with the alternatives: expose her condition and live with the consequences…

—or—

—accept this new reality and trust this presence which has just changed my life forever? Where is justice here?

But—I have dreamed; and the dream brings me light…

The decision is wrenching; but, having weighed the options, having listened to the messenger, Joseph decides on the side of mercy:

—to protect the mother

—to parent the son

—to trust against better judgment

>   —to have the courage to dream
>   beyond the fear, all the way to
>   "*YES!*"

Joseph, obedient servant of God,
with a simple YES!"
gives Mary the protection of a husband,
gives the Child the dignity of a father figure,
gives both the security of an extended family.

Joseph's message is compassion, concern,
constancy — TRUST!— yet
he never says *one word*.

Though Joseph is called to be
silent, though we never hear
his voice—yet his silent
obedience **SHOUTS!!**

*…Mary set out… in haste to
the house of Zechariah…*

THE VISIT

Mary is in a hurry!

Eager to see her cousin, she leaves immediately to journey to Zechariah's home. There's not a moment to lose; Elizabeth is pregnant!

She can't wait to hug her, to rejoice with her, to celebrate their mutual delight in anticipation of new life.

The journey is difficult: some ninety miles of rocky, uneven terrain; but Mary is carried by her joy:

—Joy for Elizabeth who waited so many years and suffered feelings of emptiness and darkness…
—Joy and anticipation because of the tiny life growing in her own womb…
—Joy that only comes from the God of surprises in the fullness of time…
—Joy: indescribable…unquenchable…overwhelming…

JOY!!!

Elizabeth sees Mary approaching, and in that moment, feels the unmistakable flutter in her womb: **LIFE!!**

She runs, arms wide open, to wrap her cousin in an embrace and greet her:

"The moment I saw you coming, the babe in my womb leapt for joy! But who am I that the mother of my Lord should come to me?"

Mary's response:
> "My whole being proclaims… *every bit* of my spirit rejoices……
> because the mighty One
> has done great things;
>
> Holy is God's name!"

When the time arrived ... Elizabeth gave birth to a son.... all heard that the Lord had shown great mercy, and they rejoiced....

JOHN

At last…
A child is born..a son!!! …so eagerly anticipated and treasured by his parents; nothing short of a miracle!

There is great celebration among the friends and relatives, and as neighbors and family members search for a name, wanting to name him after his father, his mother, Elizabeth, breaks in:
> "No. He will be called John."

All are shocked!
They argue that *no one* in the family bears that name; tradition must be served…

Zechariah takes a tablet and writes,
> "His name is John!"

…and in that moment, Zechariah's tongue is freed!
Amazement fills the room and Zechariah praises God:

"You, child, will be called the prophet of the Most High, for you will go before the Lord to prepare the way…

…to give his people knowledge of salvation through the forgiveness of sins…
…to shine on those who sit in darkness and death's shadow…
… to guide our feet into the path of peace…

Blessed be the Lord, the God of Israel!!"

*Listen to a couple seeking
shelter from the winter's cold.
Listen to the world's rejection
wandering pilgrims far from home
find a shelter
in the darkness
refuge from the world's indifference.*

JOURNEY

Cold winter night...dark, lonely road... A man and woman slowly make their way through the blackness, no moon to light their path; weary strangers on the way, journeying northward through Judean mountain wilderness toward an ancestral land.

He a poor carpenter, silent, strong— supports the woman as they struggle on the way. She, heavy with child, journeying toward her destiny's call: asking...seeking...knocking... yearning for a place to rest, to set free a life straining—*eager*—to be born.

No welcome awaits them; only another closed door as they move slowly from house to house in desperate hope of stranger's welcome. But there is no shelter to be found; the doors are locked, there is **no** room, no respite from the cold and gloom....and still they hope; because even though the journey is difficult, even though the way is long, they journey under a promise:

"GOD is with us! — we do not walk alone!"
 —and *that* is enough.

Bethlehem — only a small village... yet a ruler... will come from you, whose origin is from of old— one who will lead...in the majestic name of the Lord ...

BETHLEHEM

Bethlehem
City of David
House of bread
Birthplace of hope:
Too small, too poor, too remote, too unimportant—

Can *anything* good spring forth from
such as *you*?

Bethlehem: not much of a town, barely
deserves a dot on the map. Boasting one
traffic light and a general store, it offers
nothing that might entice a traveler to
linger awhile… not so much a destination
as a pass-through on the way to somewhere
else.

In Bethlehem, nothing noteworthy ever
seems to happen:
        But its name:
        Beth-le-hem means
        'House of Bread".

This is the place chosen by God as the
birthplace and expression of God's response
to a people hungry and fearful in the night.

This year there is a census, and any who name this as their family's origin must return and be counted

—because even in the City of David, there are taxes to be paid!

> Bethlehem
> bathed in light
> place of pilgrimage
> where strangers
> gather…
>
> Rejoice!
> for this night shall come
> forth from you
> greatness redemption

> The Holy One of Israel!

…in thy dark streets shineth the everlasting light;
the hopes and fears of all the years

are met in thee tonight…"

"There was no room…

INNKEEPER

Business had been slow; but with this census, many travelers have come seeking lodging. Tonight, we're full up! No room left at all! This is prosperity enough to provide sufficient abundance for a long time to come.

Once again, the doorbell…
I open and see there a young woman, large with child, leaning heavily on a man struggling to support her. They look exhausted, and I am moved by the sight of them.

Only a moment ago, I was celebrating the fact that my house is full; but now I wish I could offer this couple even a *small* place to rest and recover before moving on. It saddens me to think that I must turn them away when it's clear that she will give birth soon: that right now, when she needs help the most, I must tell them that I have no place for them—no offer of shelter, no relief.

Then I remember: the cave where the animals are sheltered!—not much, to be sure; but it's a roof over their heads with breath of animals to keep them warm—even a feeding trough where the baby can sleep.

I am thankful to have at least *this* to offer, and they accept gratefully.

So long ago he knocked on our door,
journeyed long and far the dusty road
to live in our hearts —
and there was no room for him.
Is there room today?
                      -or-
Do we continue to turn away—
to close our doors and miss the miracle?

Doors closed—hearts closed. It is night.
Darkness covers the earth.
We stumble blindly, not knowing what it is we seek.

Listen to the sound of birthing…
bringing forth into the light

Child of wonder, Prince of peace
crying in the wilderness:
world's salvation
hope of nations
drowning out the shouts
of war

NATIVITY

Life!
…straining to be born, eager to be freed from womb's dark confinement as the mother labors to give him life, release him to the light.

The carpenter extends strong, calloused hands, catches the tiny boy gently as he announces his arrival with a lusty wail, and for a moment holds him close before he places him into his mother's arms…

…and Mary, exhausted from her labor, still has strength enough to smile as she sees her "YES!" enfleshed.

The mother studies the child closely, marveling at the perfection of what God has created:
The Son of God?
—but he looks just like any other newborn.

He grasps her finger and she smiles, surprised at the strength of the tiny fist and the instinct that tries to carry it to his mouth.

The Son of God?
In this moment, he's just her baby boy.

The virgin wraps the baby gently, swaddles him in rags, and wonders as she places him into the manger:

> *What will his life be?*
> *What is God's plan for him? Who*
> *will he become?*

With those questions, Mary closes her eyes and surrenders to peaceful sleep…

Hail Mary, woman of courage
unconditional "Y**es**!"
strong in her weakness
submissive servant
instrument chosen

Hail Mary, homeless pilgrim
steadfast in faith
clinging to promise
silent in witness
life that proclaims

Holy Mary, Incarnation's vessel
birthing the Word in an uncaring world
cradling her newborn
holding the helpless safe in her arms

Holy Mary, refuge of pilgrims
woman of sorrow
heartbroken mother
humbly obedient
abandoned to the Will divine.

Child, wonder of birth, Why do you come here?
What is the power that brings you sends you
　　　to this place — this people?
Born today: heaven's bright promise
riding the hopes of a world lost in dark.

Life at its dawning, hope for tomorrow….

JOSEPH

Joseph, seeing Mary tired, lifts the
tiny bundle from the manger, cradles
him in strong arms, gazing in
wonder at the miracle he is:
> the soft curls, the
> curve of a cheek—
> and a BIG yawn.

It's safe and warm here, and the baby sleeps
peacefully as in a father's arms…

For a moment, does Joseph forget that this
child is not his own, but belongs completely
to God?

This child has a life and mission beyond
humanity; but for now, all Joseph can do is
drink him in with his eyes and love him with a
full heart.

He ponders:
This baby is not — never can be — mine!
But I feel as close to him as if he were. I'll
teach him and guide him, protect him and
laugh with him.

Though not my flesh, still he is gift entrusted to my care;
and I will love him as my own and dream a father's

dreams for him, and thank God for the gift of him in my arms.

Joseph swaddles the baby more closely and places him gently back into the manger.

One day years hence, another Joseph will gently wrap in clean linen the broken, lifeless body of the man this child is destined to become, and place him gently into his own new tomb.

As humanity kneels before the Infant this holy night, so it will kneel again one glorious morning…

Listen to the angels' singing:
music swells in grand crescendo;
one star glowing, leading, drawing
rich and poor to humble shelter:

shepherds' homage to the Lamb
finder of the straying lost…

SHEPHERDS

Tending our flocks on a cold, dark night, we draw our tunics closer against the biting wind. With eyes heavy with sleep, we long for the welcoming warmth of a fire.

Tonight we sense a restlessness in the flock; the sheep can't seem to settle down… we see their agitated, aimless wandering, almost as if sensing the approach of a nameless "something" — more felt than seen— unlike anything they have known. They seem to shiver with excitement as they wait…

…for…??

We watch as the brilliant light of a single star pierces the dark, brightening the sky as it journeys westward, lighting the way, urging us to follow.

Suddenly, the sound of angelic voices shatters the silence, filling the night with "Alleluia!" … "Glory to God!!… and on earth, peace!!"

"…and heaven and nature sing!"

…westward leading, still proceeding;
Guide us to thy perfect light…

MAGI

For years we have studied the ancient prophecies concerning the promise of a new king of the Jews. We've searched the heavens carefully, looking for any indication as to *when* this birth might happen. Recently, we've become aware of a *new* star, stronger and brighter than any we've seen. We wonder: is *this* the prophetic sign we've been anticipating? Is this the announcement that soon will be born a new king of the Jews? If not, what *other* sign should we look for?

It's because of this that Herod has summoned us; he wants to know *exactly* when the star appeared, and any other relevant details we might be able to provide. We respond as best we can according to the information we have so far; and as we prepare to leave his presence, Herod orders us to "…search carefully… report back to me so that I too may go and worship him."

We resume our journey, studying the heavens as we go, and watching the star closely. The attraction is so great, the star so brilliant, that even though we don't know where the journey will take us, we journey *for the sake of the journey,* certain that we will know the place when we arrive.

Finally, the star comes to rest over a cave.
A cave??
Did we expect something else?

Not sure whether this is our destination, and having nothing to go on but the fact that the star has come to a stop, we look around to see what else is in the area that might offer a clue; but there is nothing — just this cave.

We enter; and there we see an infant in the arms of his mother—and *we know!!*

We fall to our knees in worship, realizing that we are in the presence of the Prophecy fulfilled: the enfleshment of our hopes, and the salvation of *all* people.

Here, in this place, before our eyes—is the Promise!!

We have brought gifts for the new baby King, and we present them:

Gold: symbol of divinity associated with earthly kingship; to acknowledge his royalty

Frankincense: fragrant spice used in offering sacrifice; to acknowledge his priesthood

Myrrh: spice used for embalming; symbol of pain, suffering, death; to foreshadow his martyrdom.

Herod has commanded us to return with information surrounding the birth of this new infant King..but, having found the place of the birth, having seen with our own eyes and worshipped the wonder of the Child in the cave, we are transformed.

Warned in a dream about Herod's intent, we resolve to return by another path.

> Because we have dreamed…
> because we have worshipped…
> because we believe…
> we will *never* be the same.
> we *must* find another way home…

Slowly they approach: the wealthy, the lowly the homeless, the strays all people and all creatures together kneel in silence before a child wreathed in light born to rescue us from night.

We…chosen people..
still we seek you
still we wander in the darkness we create.
Lead us in our wandering …

across the desert
through the cold
teach us once again to hope
as we kneel again before your majesty
in a humble cave bathed in light…

HEROD

Although referred to in the Bible as "King Herod" and "Herod the Great", the Herod of this account is Herod Antipas, one of the four *sons* of Herod the Great: a tetrarch whose power extends to only about *one-fourth* of the realm, making him a lesser authority with delusions of greatness.

Though he imagines himself, and claims to be, a king, the idea of a new King is threatening, because his insecurity and lust for power are all he can see. So the Magi's visit is unsettling enough to send him into a major tantrum.

"What is this news? I've heard the whispers, the undercurrent of excited claims that a new king is coming....

—but—

THERE IS NO KING BUT ME !!
I am Herod — **the GREAT!!**
I am the king:
>> the strong— the
>> absolute—
>> monarch.

Let *no one* think that he can take MY place! Let no one try, with might or artifice, to claim what is mine, and mine alone!!

Let this new "king" come before me and show himself! Let him stand and face me, and declare that *he* is mightier than I!

I *must* find out about this so-called "king":
Where does he come from?
What is his lineage?
What makes him think he can depose *me*?
What is the kingdom he presumes to claim?

A KING?!!

We'll just see about that!!"

"Oh come, all ye faithful…"

PILGRIMS

Our journey has taught us, inspired us, drawn us to the place where we now stand. Guided by the Star, we find ourselves at the entrance to a cave, with Gabriel waiting to open the way in for us. The Star hovers overhead as we enter.

At first our eyes need a moment to adjust to the darkness within; but eyesight gradually clears, and we are able to discern a soft light around what appears to be a crude manger. Slowly we become aware of a couple holding and playing with a baby.

Could *this* be the One?

Having not known what to expect, we are surprised by the simplicity of the setting, the "ordinary"-ness of the Child and these parents, who seem like any other young family: nothing exceptional, but somehow strongly magnetic.

The Baby looks away from his parents, and our eyes meet. What is this feeling? It's as if I've just encountered someone *very* important, whose power is undisputed….
        But—this is a baby!

How can I explain exactly what I see —
 how I feel?

࿇࿇࿇࿇

Hand that created a universe
fashioned a humanity out of clay
fingers that knit me in my mother's womb
wrap themselves firmly around a mother's own.

Voice that called forth all that lives
called Abraham and Moses
forged a covenant with an unholy people
voice that is thunder and music
power and authority—
coos and gurgles in the warm safety
of a mother's arms.

Eyes that visioned the perfection of a sunset
saw mountains' grandeur and oceans' power
eyes that saw me before I came to be
look up from a feeding trough
into my face:
baby eyes, full of innocence
and trust
ancient eyes, deep and full of wisdom.

Feet that trod the expanse of Eden
walked with Adam in the cool
journeyed through a desert forty years—
these tiny, perfect, unscarred feet—
where will they take you, child of grace?

Pillar of cloud and smoke
leading a people out of slavery
power of wind and storm and flood—
calmer of seas, painter of the rainbow
heart of compassion broken by betrayal
searching still to embrace and forgive.

All this rests in a feeding trough:
a baby, wrapped in rags
and warmed by breath of animals
waits for the "yes" my breath will form.

This paradox before us:
the King of kings   our
only hope:

Emmanuel!

We leave that sacred place transformed, knowing
we will never be the same…

There was in Jerusalem a man whose name was Simeon. It had been revealed ...that he would not see death before he had seen the Messiah ...

SIMEON

Old man waiting in the temple, relying on the hope: God's promise made so long ago that in his lifetime, he would see Salvation born.

Now, as days grow short for him, he still remembers the promise…still looks forward to the promise, always clinging to the expectation that God's word *can* be trusted, *will* be fulfilled— in God's time… and he waits in joyful hope… praying as he has every day for so many years:

"Lord, I have waited so long. I am old and tired, and the days left to me are few. I have been patient, knowing that you always keep your promises; and so I still wait and still hope, resting in your faithful love."

Just then, Simeon sees a couple enter the temple, the woman cradling in her arms a baby son. She approaches in silence, head bowed; and Simeon recognizes that
>*this* mother…*this* child…
>are God's promise — enfleshed!

The mother gently places the child into Simeon's arms. The old man gazes into the infant's eyes, his own wet with tears; and with grateful, joy-filled heart, he blesses the God of Promise:

"Now that my eyes have seen, my arms have held, I desire no more. Life now complete, your servant, Lord, is ready to depart in peace; for I have seen, and now I hold
>
> Salvation in my arms."

Lowering his voice, he speaks to the mother: "This child will be a contradiction; because of him, many will rise and many will fall; and as hearts are revealed, your own heart will be pierced…"

…and Mary listens…and ponders…

ANNA

I came to the temple as a young widow and have lived here ever since then. I've spent these many years fasting, praying, poring over ancient Scripture, and studying the signs of the times: always believing, anticipating— never doubting for a moment that *this day* would come.

A little while ago, I saw a young family enter the temple, watched as the mother placed the infant into Simeon's arms. I saw his tears and listened as he prayed his gratitude and blessing to the God of Promise…

…and *I knew!!*

Coming forward at this very moment, I announced to all present the wonderful news that *this* child is indeed the long-awaited Promised One, thus revealing the connection between the Promise and its Fulfillment.

And all who heard this rejoiced and celebrated!

HEROD

Time has passed since the visit of the Magi, and Herod is restless: where are the astrologers who were commanded to report back to me? Why has there been no word from them?

Slowly he comes to believe that he has been tricked; that the three *never* intended to return with news of the newborn King.

So angry, so full of outrage, he summons his soldiers and gives the command: "Find all of the male children under two years old, and

KILL…..THEM…..ALL!!
I AM THE KING OF THE JEWS!!

…and the sound of mourning and bitter weeping is heard throughout the countryside as babies are slaughtered without mercy until no boy-child remains…
　—potential extinguished—
　—parental hopes and dreams shattered —
and then— silence: no sound of children playing, no hope for lives denied by *one* man's viciousness…

GABRIEL

Joseph!

JOSEPH!!

Wake up!! Get up *right now!*— and wake Mary and the Child!!

It's no longer safe for you here!
Herod is on a rampage and has commanded his army to seek out all the baby boys under two years old

    —and KILL THEM!!

You *must* leave immediately! Take your family to Egypt, where you will be protected. Remain there until you are told that the danger is past.

   LEAVE…NOW!!! ***HURRY!!***

…and Joseph obeyed….
quickly gathered their few belongings, awakened Mary and the Child, and without a word, led them out of the cave's shelter into the night, toward safe refuge in Egypt…

PILGRIMS

The people described in this telling are very much like all of us: prone to question and doubt, slow to grasp, but still willing to learn. These are the very ones God has chosen to tell the Story: imperfect humans, entrusted with the fine crystal. But the story isn't fragile. The story is timeless: always new though well-known; always fresh through generations of telling and re-telling; always *our* story, gifted to us by the Author.

We have journeyed together this adventure: watching, learning — caring for one another as we've traveled. We've met the Story through the people who have *lived* the Story; and we're moved by the trust that God places in mere humans. Also moving is the story *we've* lived on the way as we have seen for ourselves the unfolding of:

Mary's obedience and Joseph's support; Elizabeth's patience and Zechariah's silence, the innkeeper's compassion, the shepherds' curiosity, the Magi's persistent searching, the martyred babies, Simeon's steadfast faithfulness to the Promise, and Anna's public declaration of faith.

Like the Magi, we have dreamed, we have worshipped, we believe… and now we return home, forever changed.

ೆೊೊೊ

But the Promise we see in its fullness
only proves to our eyes and our hearts
that our deepest of reachings
our wildest of yearnings
have simply not been wild enough.

On that great day we met our Hope
born in a cave in Bethlehem. New
life sprung forth from hopes we
thought had died. The long wait
ended, our deepest longings
satisfied:
> covenant born
> promise kept—

all came to rest in the gloom of a cave made
bright by the Child of the Promise:

> Wrapped in justice.
> girded in peace.
> holding out baby arms.
> offering shalom.

All this in one word:

Emmanuel!

—conceived   from   the   very   beginning
> deep in God's imagination.

…and the Light shines on in the darkness…

ACKNOWLEDGEMENTS

As I've learned, it takes more than one person working alone to create anything of value. This is especially true when an aspiring author sets out to pull thoughts together in the hope of emerging with something akin to the "greatest story ever told".

I wanted to capture the Christmas story as I've never heard it expressed; because sometimes it seems that, in the rush and excitement of *preparation* for the Big Day, people lose sight of the *reason* for the Big Day. So I asked the people who actually *lived* the story to tell me in their own words what it was like to be chosen to participate in such an endeavor. This work is the result of those conversations— an opportunity to see God at work in God's people.

Of course, I have not done this alone; many, with or without realizing it, have helped me pull the story together into the work you holds in your hand

So I give thanks….

First, to God, who gives me the words and the means to express them;

...to Fr. Patrick Zengierski: who reviewed, supported, suggested—and then stepped aside;

...to Fr. James Daprile, who caught details I missed, and offered input in presenting and clarifying them;

...to Faye Luckett, my editor, whose knowledge and devotion I treasure, as she walked with me through the process with a fine-toothed comb, and reviewed meticulously the final draft — always affirming and supporting;

...to all of *you* who have asked, wondered when, and encouraged...

Finally, to Ron, who patiently read and reread, who held me accountable, and who celebrates *with* me and *for* me any small success I may achieve —never imagining that *he* — *his support*—is my strength and my secret weapon!

Sylvia Dains

www.ingramcontent.com/pod-product-compliance
Lightning Source LLC
Chambersburg PA
CBHW071510070526
44578CB00001B/497